Original title:
Through the Whispering Woods

Copyright © 2025 Creative Arts Management OÜ
All rights reserved.

Author: Mariana Leclair
ISBN HARDBACK: 978-1-80567-341-5
ISBN PAPERBACK: 978-1-80567-640-9

The Lingering Calm of Twilight

The squirrels chatter, oh what a sight,
As shadows stretch with fading light.
A raccoon winks, perched high on a limb,
While fireflies dance with a glow so dim.

The owl hoots jokes about the day,
As crickets join in, leading the way.
A chipmunk chuckles, tucked in a nook,
While all the trees wear a comical look.

Beneath the Skyward Spires

Beneath the tall trees that tickle the sky,
A parrot squawks riddles, oh me, oh my!
A badger in spectacles reads a tall tale,
While the sun sneezes clouds in a whimsical gale.

The wind blows softly, with giggles and glee,
As the pine cones drop with a clatter and spree.
A family of deer holds a dance-off so grand,
With rabbits as judges, it's quite the demand!

A Fairytale Among the Ferns

In a land where the ferns wore funny hats,
A clever fox traded tall tales with the cats.
A frog with a crown croaked songs of the past,
While the flowers applauded, oh how they laughed!

The butterflies twirled in a dizzying spree,
As they played hide and seek with a hummingbee.
A snail with a tie held court on a leaf,
Declaring that laughter is the best kind of relief.

The Call of the Wildflower Trail

Upon a trail where wildflowers sway,
A bear shares gossip on this sunny day.
The daisies nod, with a chuckle and cheer,
While a hedgehog recites poetry near.

A bunny, quite posh, sips tea in the shade,
Discussing the latest in berry brigade.
With laughter and joy, the forest will sing,
For each little creature brings forth quirky things.

Sighs Between Light and Leaf

The sun peeks and gives a grin,
While squirrels plot their next big win.
A chatty bird mimics my shoe,
Saying, "That's a bold look for you!"

The leaves sway as if in cheer,
"I swear I saw a bear right here!"
But all that's left of that brave dream,
Is just a bush and a sunbeam.

Tales Carved in Old Trunks

A wise old owl told me a tale,
About a frog that learned to sail.
He wore a hat that was too big,
And danced a jig with quite a swig!

Beneath the bark, a mouse did plot,
To steal some cheese from a long-forgot.
But tripping on a wayward twig,
He found himself doing a jig!

The Dance of Dust and Dew

At dawn, the dust begins to twirl,
While raindrops laugh and start to swirl.
A ladybug joins in the fray,
Saying, "I'll show you how to play!"

With every step they stomp and hop,
And squirrels laugh until they drop.
The grass joins in, a swaying crowd,
"Who knew the woods could be so loud?"

Beneath the Brooding Boughs

Beneath the boughs where shadows fall,
A raccoon tries to walk tall.
He trips and tumbles, lands with flair,
"Who needs style when you've got hair?"

The whispers tease the branches sway,
"Oi, watch your steps!" they seem to say.
But laughter swirls, an endless song,
In this wild world where all belong.

Fragments of Dream Among the Trees

In the forest, squirrels dance,
Chasing shadows, taking a chance.
A raccoon wears an acorn hat,
While the fox giggles, how about that!

A rabbit jokes in his own way,
Spinning tales of a leafy ballet.
The owl hoots, it's quite absurd,
Claiming wisdom, but misheard!

Underneath the starry twinkle,
A porcupine tries not to crinkle.
With every step, he gives a poke,
Oh, the laughter, it just won't choke!

So raise a toast with a twig by chance,
To all the creatures who love to dance.
In this wood of dreams and fun,
The wildest tales have just begun!

The Ballet of Blades and Mist

Mice in tutu, prance around,
Dancing on the frosty ground.
While the badger plays the flute,
All amazed by his furry suit!

The trees clap hands, or so it seems,
At the critters' zany dreams.
A turtle turns, takes two steps back,
Oops! Down went the lion snack!

Leaves swirl in a pirouette,
A comical sight, can't forget.
The hedgehog twirls, a masterclass,
With every spin, he shakes his grass!

Under the moon, they end the show,
All the creatures, putting on a glow.
With a bow, they wink and grin,
In this forest, fun's a win!

An Ode to the Swaying Spirits

Ghosts in pajamas float and sway,
In the trees, they come out to play.
They trip on branches, giggling loud,
Making mischief, feeling proud!

A glow-worm leads a conga line,
The mushrooms join, each one divine.
The haunted breeze sings funny tunes,
As fireflies light the way to noon!

The spirits dance, they've lost their chill,
Chasing shadows, bending will.
A friendly ghost makes a pie,
Then drops it—oh my! Oh my!

Amidst the laughter, all collide,
In this twilight, they take pride.
For every giggle, every ghost,
Here's to fun—let's raise a toast!

Moonlit Pathways of Serenity

A raccoon danced with glee,
Its tail a twirling streak.
The owls laughed with delight,
As fireflies began to peek.

A squirrel threw a nut,
Missed the tree by a mile.
The rabbits giggled loud,
Each with a cheeky smile.

The moonlight played a tune,
Bouncing off the leaves.
Foxes pranced and leaped,
In their midnight thieves.

So if you wander here,
Watch for antics show!
The night is full of jest,
With critters head to toe.

The Laughter of Leafy Shadows

The shadows stretched and yawned,
A breeze giggled near.
Quiet whispers of the trees,
Made woodland jokes clear.

A skunk plays peekaboo,
With a bashful little grin.
"Don't mind the smell!" it said,
As the others started to spin.

Chirps and chuckles filled the air,
The night hummed with cheer.
A badger tried to dance,
And tripped over a deer.

Howling winds chimed in,
With a funny little quirk.
In every nook and cranny,
Laughter lived at work.

Beneath the Veil of Green

A turtle stole a hat,
From a nearby lazy cat.
And while the cat just blinked,
The turtle thought it flat.

Parrots squawked a tune,
About a chubby toad.
"Have you seen my dinner?"
"Maybe it's on the road!"

The fawns played hide and seek,
But fell into a bog.
"Moo!" said a passing cow,
As they waved a soggy log.

Life beneath the green,
Is laughter day and night.
With antics so absurd,
Both furry and polite.

Murmurs of the Ancient Trees

The trees began to chat,
In a language all their own.
"Did you hear that squirrel?"
"No, but I saw it moan!"

An ant complained about,
A long and winding route.
While butterflies just giggled,
And floated all about.

The breeze chimed in with jokes,
Making leaves shake and sway.
With every hearty laugh,
The night turned into day.

So if you stop to hear,
The wise trees' funny lore,
You might just find yourself,
Rolling on the forest floor.

The Forest's Hidden Heart

In a forest green with glee,
Squirrels dance on tiptoes free.
A rabbit hops, wearing a hat,
Shouting, "I'm late! For tea! How 'bout that?"

Under trees that sway and sway,
Frogs sing songs of a rainy day.
A wise old owl plays chess at night,
With a raccoon who cheats—what a sight!

Glimpses of Eden's Breath

A fox with style, a spiffy tie,
Claims he's the king; he's rather spry.
Beneath a bush, a turtle jokes,
While crafty birds steal crumbs from folks.

A dance-off starts with swirling leaves,
As ants join in, wearing tiny sleeves.
Even the flowers chuckle and sway,
Singing, "Join us all, it's a silly day!"

The Labyrinth of Leafy Secrets

In this maze of green and brown,
A snail with dreams weighs a million pounds.
He slides along, a gourmet chef,
Cooking up plans for all the rest.

A hedgehog prances, quite a sight,
With pom-poms made of dandelion light.
The whispers of twigs play little tricks,
As laughter echoes, oh what a mix!

The Spirit of the Hushed Grove

Deep in quiet, where shadows tease,
Lies a monster made of fluffy cheese.
It rolls and laughs, it bounces high,
As butterflies join, and giggle by.

The trees wear smiles, their branches bend,
As a gopher comes, seeking a friend.
They toss their worries to the breeze,
In this place of joy, everyone's pleased!

Air Thick with Forgotten Tales

Once a squirrel wore a hat,
He danced around and sat.
The trees all shook with glee,
As birds sang with crazy glee.

A frog joined in the fun,
With jokes that never run.
He leapt from branch to branch,
While bugs began to dance.

A rabbit baked a pie,
But forgot it made him cry.
He spilled it on the ground,
And every critter frowned.

The breeze began to laugh,
As nature wrote a blurb.
With every giggle shared,
The world had grown absurd!

A Prelude to the Woodland Dream

There's a snail who tells tall tales,
He claims to ride on gales.
Among the ants he sits,
While sharing wild little bits.

A hedgehog makes a soup,
With mushrooms in a loop.
It bubbled like a song,
Yet tasted all wrong!

A beetle plays the flute,
With leaves his only loot.
The mushrooms began to sway,
In their hilarious way!

A chipmunk joined the band,
With acorns in his hand.
Together they performed,
As nature laughed and swarmed!

Nature's Lullaby in the Gloom

In the dusky evening shade,
A sloth tried to masquerade.
He wore a hat too big,
And danced a silly jig.

The owls hooted with delight,
As raccoons joined the night.
With giggles, they took flight,
What a curious sight!

A fox began to snore,
While critters sought for more.
They tiptoed past his den,
And let the fun begin!

Beneath the starry skies,
A rabbit swapped his pies.
With laughter in the breeze,
Nature's lullabies tease!

The Rustling of Silent Sighs

There's a mouse who tells sweet lies,
About shadows that can fly.
He says the grass can giggle,
And even start to wiggle.

A crow dunked in a stream,
Thought he was a dream.
He flapped his wings in vain,
As bubbles caused him pain.

A bumblebee wore shoes,
Claimed he could never lose.
He buzzed and made a fuss,
While flowers joined with us.

From the earth, the laughs would rise,
Nature's whispers in disguise.
And in this merry land,
All creatures formed a band!

Sylvan Secrets Unveiled

In a forest of giggles, the squirrels take flight,
Chasing their tails in the soft morning light.
A fox in a tuxedo, quite dapper, it seems,
Winks at the rabbits, all lost in their dreams.

Mice on roller skates zoom past a tall pine,
While owls serve tea, both amusing and fine.
Each tree has a story, each leaf has a laugh,
As shadows play tag in their own leafy craft.

A bear with a bowtie, so silly and round,
Dances to rhythms that only he's found.
With berries for snacks and laughter to share,
Nature's a party, if you just stop and stare.

So if ever you wander where the wild ones play,
Join in the fun, don't be shy; come and stay!
The woods hold their secrets, both funny and bright,
Wrapped in a giggle, a sheer pure delight.

Shadows Dancing with Twilight

As dusk drapes its cloak, shadows wiggle in glee,
Dance like the fireflies, all wild and free.
Ants with their banter march up to the beat,
A conga line forms, oh, isn't it sweet?

A possum in glasses recites a great tale,
Of cheese, mighty quests, and a bold little snail.
The moon chuckles softly, gives stars a quick poke,
While critters below share a ticklish joke.

The fox teaches everyone a jig to enjoy,
While owls hoot the chorus, oh what a ploy!
The trees bend and sway, a quirky ballet,
As laughter erupts from the shadows at play.

In this twilight hush, where shadows convene,
Find joy in the funny, where life feels serene.
Join in the dance, feel the warmth of the night,
Where silliness glimmers, endless delight.

Beneath the Veil of Leaves

Beneath leaves that rustle, secrets unfurl,
A crab in a dance and a snail with a twirl.
Mushrooms wear hats, oh, what a fine sight,
While crickets throw parties with lanterns so bright.

A deer plays the violin, serenades the pines,
Twigs clap in rhythm, bobbing in lines.
Foxes with fedoras debate on the best,
While badgers munch popcorn, enjoying the jest.

Each bush has a chuckle, each brook sings along,
A frog in a tutu, he can't get it wrong.
With laughter and music, they frolic and play,
In this leafy wonder, they brighten the day.

So wander if you can to this realm that is free,
Where nature reveals its comedic esprit.
Embrace all the joy that this haven conceals,
In the playful embrace of the vibrant green reels.

The Soft Serenade of Trees

The trees softly chuckle, their branches in sway,
As birds join the chorus, making fun play.
A caterpillar croons a whimsical tune,
While ants practice ballet beneath the bright moon.

A nut falls with giggles, a jesting old tale,
Of squirrels in top hats who sail on a gale.
Pinecones play poker, the stakes are quite high,
While fireflies blink their little 'hi-fi'.

The breeze carries whispers, a snicker, a cheer,
While mushrooms are painting, oh what a fun circle here!

And hedgehogs are giggling as they roll down the hill,
Creating a ruckus, what a beautiful thrill!

So listen, dear wanderer, if you chance to stroll,
The trees hold the laughter, a magical soul.
In this comedy show of earth, sky, and glee,
Nature wins the spotlight, amusingly free.

The Faery's Breath

In a glen where faeries prance,
They giggle and they dance.
With wings that sparkle bright,
They steal socks in the night.

Mushrooms giggle, flowers greet,
With tiny shoes upon their feet.
They tickle noses passing by,
While hiding from a curious eye.

When moonlight spills a silver glow,
The faeries gather, start the show.
They play pranks with a little flare,
Painting stones and switching hair.

So if you hear a little squeak,
It's just the faeries playing peek.
Beware the giggles, don't be late,
Or you just might become their mate!

Rustling Secrets Beneath the Stars

Beneath the twinkling night so clear,
The critters whisper, 'Come in here!'
A squirrel juggles acorns with cheer,
While a raccoon plays the tambourine near.

A wise old owl tells silly jokes,
As hedgehogs laugh and tease the folks.
With twinkling eyes, they share their dreams,
Of cake-filled trees and chocolate streams.

The wind carries tales on its breath,
Of dancing mice that make no mess.
They tap their tiny feet in time,
As fireflies light the night with rhyme.

Every rustle holds a secret laugh,
The forest is a fanciful gaffe.
So join the fun and shed your cares,
For mischief flies in nightly flares!

Echoes of the Untold

In a realm where shadows play,
Old stories sneak and sway.
A fox dressed up in a cape of grass,
Whispers secrets as the squirrels pass.

Behind the trees, a gnome does snooze,
Wakes with a start, "Who's wearing my shoes?"
With laughter echoing, he chases them fast,
While the rabbits clap, having a blast.

An owl hoots a tune quite absurd,
A serenade to every bird.
With disco balls made of dew,
They dance around till the day is new.

In every corner, giggles bloom,
As the stars wink in the forest's room.
So listen close, and you might find,
Timeless tales of a funny kind!

Enigma of the Twilight Wood

In the twilight, where shadows creep,
Woodland creatures can't help but leap.
A bear in pajamas runs in a race,
While the bunnies giggle, covering their face.

A raccoon with a hat starts to prance,
Encouraging all to join in the dance.
The trees sway gently, shaking their fruit,
As frogs in tuxedos chime in to root.

With jests and jigs, the night takes flight,
As fireflies buzz, bringing delight.
A hedgehog juggles nuts with glee,
The quirkiest show you ever did see!

As laughter bounces off each bark,
In this wood, there's always a spark.
So join the fun, let worries cease,
For every step brings giggles and peace!

The Song of the Midnight Trees

In the stillness, branches sway,
A squirrel dances, come what may.
With twinkling lights they try to weave,
A riddle most hard to believe.

Beneath the moon, the shadows prance,
The owls hoot loud, as if in trance.
The leaves conspire, giggles abound,
In leafy whispers, secrets found.

Frogs croak loudly, a choir of glee,
While fireflies flicker, can't you see?
The wind sings softly, jokes in tow,
As trees throw shade at those below.

So laugh along, let worries cease,
In nature's jest, we find our peace.
With every rustle, life's a jest,
The midnight trees know humor best.

Veils of Mist and Memory

A misty veil hides all the fun,
Where rabbits race—who's underdone?
They hop like crazed, wild little sprites,
In morning's glow, they spark delight.

The fog rolls in, a blanket cheap,
While bunnies plan their grand old leap.
"Who spooked the cabbage?" one does shout,
The answer lost in giggles stout.

A ghostly squirrel, handsome in gray,
Claims he just saw a dance today.
With acorns tossed, the game begins,
As laughter echoes 'neath the sins.

So in the mist, let's spin the yarn,
Of woodland tales, both bright and bizarre.
For in these woods where memories roam,
The funny whispers feel like home.

The Embrace of Evergreen Serenity

The pines stand tall with arms so wide,
And tickle the starlit sky with pride.
A hedgehog jokes, "I'm spiky, but sweet!"
The forest roars with laughter, oh what a treat!

The daylight fades, and critters spark,
A dance begins, igniting the dark.
The owlets tease, with winks and coos,
"Who stole my snacks?" in playful blues.

Amidst the trunks, the giggles flow,
As whispers hide in shadows low.
A merry jaunt in emerald hues,
Echoes of joy in all that they do.

So let us sway in sweet embrace,
Where laughter leads, we find our place.
In evergreen laughter, life's a song,
United in joy, where we belong.

Tides of Green and Gold

Beneath the branches, colors dance,
A bumblebee takes a funny chance.
"Excuse me, ma'am, is this your leaf?"
The flowers giggle in wild disbelief.

Dandelions wink with yellow cheer,
While ants parade, their path so clear.
A quizzical frog croaks, "What's the fuss?"
"Are we the stars?" they laugh, "Who'd discuss?"

As golden hues weave through the green,
Squirrels scamper, all sharp and keen.
"A stash of nuts?" they holler and hoot,
While not a single one is mute.

In these jewels of earth, let's find our beat,
From cheers of bugs to the glossy beet.
For in this tide, of colors bold,
Life's a romp, both bright and gold.

The Solstice of Sighs

Beneath the sun's silly grin,
The trees start to joke and spin,
A squirrel trips over a root,
While a bird laughs, dressed in a suit.

The shadows dance on the ground,
A poodle lost, and then he's found,
A rabbit hops on a cat's head,
While everyone laughs at the bread!

The flowers gossip in the breeze,
About a snail who sneezes,
A bear wearing candy-striped socks,
And a porcupine playing with rocks.

The moon joins in, a shiny ball,
Whispers secrets to us all,
In this garden, fun takes flight,
Laughter echoes through the night.

Lullabies of the Twilight Canopy

As the sun dips low in the sky,
The owls wear glasses, oh my,
A raccoon juggles acorns with flair,
While giggling leaves dance in the air.

Crickets try to sing in tune,
But they keep getting lost in the moon,
A hedgehog's hat flies off in a breeze,
Chasing after it with such ease!

The stars start to wink and tease,
As fireflies join in with a squeeze,
Shadows playing peekaboo,
As nighttime whispers, "I see you!"

In this twilight, mischief stirs,
With talking rocks and furry furs,
A night of laughter, pure delight,
Lullabies sweet, under starlight.

Tangles of Time and Tales Untold

Once there was a clock so sly,
It tick-tocked backwards, oh my,
A turtle raced, or so it aimed,
While the rabbit looked shocked and ashamed!

The trees exchanged their happy laughs,
Playing jokes on surrounding staffs,
A fox wore a funny little hat,
Dancing with a very large cat.

Leaves rustle tales of shoes gone rogue,
A hedgehog rolling down a bog,
Time slips and slides, a wacky ride,
With boisterous critters dancing side by side.

Every twist, a fresh surprise,
While bees wear ties that hypnotize,
In this tangle of giggles and fun,
The stories bloom, never done.

The Enchanted Hideaway

In a nook where giggles thrive,
A gopher gives a high-five,
The flowers snicker, while frogs croak,
As the trees shake hands and joke.

A pixie lost her way to lunch,
Found a berry and started to munch,
While a squirrel wore a tutu bright,
Twisting and twirling, what a sight!

The air is thick with playful cheer,
A dancing fern winks, "Come here!"
Stars giggle in the softest glow,
As crickets put on quite a show.

So in this hideaway, come play,
With silly friends where laughter stays,
Each moment sparkles, bright and gay,
Where fun and folly lead the way.

The Murmurs of Hidden Trails

In bushes small, a squirrel pranced,
He wore a hat, by chance, by chance.
His friends all laughed, a sight to see,
As acorns rolled, quite wild and free.

A rabbit danced, with shoes too tight,
He tripped and flipped, what a delight!
The birds all chirped their silly tunes,
As leaves fell down, like little spoons.

The shadows chuckled, trees did lean,
At every twist, a silly scene.
The wind it whispered, jokes abound,
With giggles echoing all around.

So take a stroll on paths unknown,
Where every step breaks up the stone.
For nature's jesters roam with glee,
In hidden trails, we're wild and free.

Nature's Choir Amidst the Shadows

A frog on stage, he starts to sing,
His voice so loud, it makes birds cling.
With every note, the crickets play,
A symphony in bright array.

The trees sway gently, join the fun,
As squirrels nod to beats they run.
The mushrooms giggle, sway with flair,
Each note a tickle, bouncing air.

The whispering breeze adds harmony,
While ants march proud, a tiny spree.
The clouds above drop jokes like rain,
And nature laughs, forgets the pain.

A laughter chorus fills the glade,
Amidst the shadows, bright parade.
Come join the fun, and sing along,
In nature's choir, we all belong.

The Language of the Forest Floor

The leaves all whisper silly tales,
Of owls in capes and tiny snails.
A hedgehog waves with tiny arms,
His prickly shield its own great charms.

The flowers gossip, colors bright,
About the bees that dance at night.
A squirrel quips, a funny joke,
With every cackle, branches choke.

The mushrooms giggle, join the chat,
While toads debate the flat or fat.
They gather near a bubbling brook,
For stories shared, all nature's book.

On this rich floor, all jokes unfold,
In every shade, their laughter bold.
Let's listen close, with hearts that soar,
To humor found on nature's floor.

Beneath the Watchful Eyes of Pines

Beneath tall trees, a dance did start,
A walrus waltzed, a funny art.
The pine cone clapped, a raucous cheer,
As laughter floated, warm and clear.

Two raccoons jived, their tails like whips,
With wiggly moves and comic flips.
The owls hooted, "That's quite a show!"
As shadows stretched, the moon's soft glow.

The branches bobbed to rhythmic beats,
While critters joined with furry feet.
They played charades, the stakes were high,
As laughter rang beneath the sky.

With every step on piney trails,
The hidden humor never fails.
So join the fun, and do not pine,
For every giggle, here's a sign.

Echoes of the Enchanted Grove

The squirrels chatter, plotting a heist,
While owls debate who's the wisest of mice.
A raccoon in a scarf, quite posh and spry,
Steals a picnic basket, oh my, oh my!

Beneath the tall trees, a dance breaks out,
The ferns are convinced they can twirl about.
While mushrooms giggle, saying, "Look at me!"
It's a woodland cabaret, wild and free!

Bunnies hop in tuxedos, looking so grand,
They've got monocles too, isn't that planned?
The brook starts clapping with a splash, splash, splash,
As the breeze joins in with a giggly crash.

So if you're feeling down, take a stroll,
Among playful creatures, they'll make you whole.
In the grove of echoes where laughter reigns,
Silly adventures are found in the lanes.

Secrets Beneath the Canopy

Under the leaves, secrets unfold,
A butterfly whispers, "Hey, want to be bold?"
A shy hedgehog giggles, peeking from moss,
While the chipmunks spin tales of their boss.

The raccoons are chefs, cooking up stew,
With acorns and berries, that's tried and true.
The frogs croak a tune, but it's offbeat,
Just hopping around on their tiny webbed feet.

A crow with a beret thinks he's quite slick,
While the owls roll their eyes at his old magic trick.
The trees shake their branches, laughing aloud,
As the forest creatures tumble, forming a crowd.

But shush! What's that? A fox sneezing near,
Echoes of laughter, they quiver in fear.
Beneath the great canopy, fun's never shy,
In the secret of woodland, humor is nigh.

Whispers of Moss and Moonlight

The mushrooms give gossip, hidden in hue,
While fireflies dance, saying, "Look at you!"
The raccoons wear shades, at a moonlit show,
Dancing under stars in a glow like a pro.

The snails are slow, but they've got a groove,
Sliding on ferns, making their move.
The owls are the judges, hooting for fun,
As crickets audition, all hoping to run.

The vines are the curtains, swaying with grace,
Each creature a player in this grand space.
But oh! What's that? A badger forgot,
His lines in the script, now he stands there in thought.

Laughter fills the air, the moon smiles wide,
Even branches are shaking, can't hold their pride.
In the realm of shadows, where giggles loom,
Moss and moonlight spread joy like a room full of bloom.

The Path Beneath the Ancient Bark

Beneath the old trees, a trail we find,
Where foxes act silly, and owls are unkind.
A hedgehog in sneakers rolls by in a rush,
Chased by a rabbit, who's causing a hush.

The jokes of the toadstools fly high in the air,
Making the beetles roll over in despair.
As the leaves start to giggle, the branches sway,
Whispering secrets of the antics at play.

The breeze carries laughter from one end to the next,
While the crows on a branch critique with respect.
"Your dance is quite charming but lacks a good flair,"
They caw and they cackle, a humorous pair.

So come take a stroll, let your worries depart,
In the woods full of laughter, where joy fills the heart.
The path beneath bark, where stories are spun,
Is a canvas of giggles, let's join in the fun!

A Reverie in the Glade

In the glade, a squirrel pranced,
Scoffing at the fox who danced.
"You think you're sly?" he chattered loud,
"I've seen you trip; you're not so proud!"

Beneath the shade of towering trees,
A rabbit snickered at the bees.
"You buzz around like chatty folks,
But can't dodge raindrops? Oh, what jokes!"

A deer with antlers, grand and wide,
Was startled by a frog that cried.
"You think you own this lively scene?"
"With such a leap, you're hardly seen!"

The wise old owl perched on a branch,
Giggled softly at the monkey's dance.
"You swing so high, but watch your tail,
You might just miss that blackberry pale!"

Echoes of the Forgotten Path

On the path where all shoes disappear,
A raccoon exclaimed, "Hey, not over here!"
"The snacks you dropped are long gone now,
You must have danced without a vow!"

A wise old tortoise passed me slow,
Mumbling tales of a once-great show.
"I had my time, oh yes, I did,
But now I just wander, lovably hid!"

A hedgehog giggled in a thorny bed,
"Your maps are useless, go home instead!"
"For nature's path is crazy and wild,
And we all laugh like a happy child!"

When the pathway chuckled with delight,
Even owls hooted at the quirky sight.
"If you're lost, just dance with the breeze,
Laughter fills the air with such sweet ease!"

Secrets in the Silent Grove

In a grove where secrets lie deep,
Laughed a gnome who never would sleep.
"Shh! Don't tell the others, it's a treat,
But I snuck in here for a nice, warm seat!"

A chatter of birds started to squawk,
"What's the secret? We heard your talk!"
The gnome, in a flash, hid his face,
"Only if you promise, no rat race!"

The groundhog popped from his tiny hole,
Said, "You appear to lack your soul."
He rolled on the grass, ventured a tease,
"You're more amusing than a summer breeze!"

The pets all gathered, curious and bold,
For the secrets the gnome would unfold.
But with a wink and a chuckle so sly,
He vanished, leaving just a goofy sigh!

Echoes Beneath the Canopy

Beneath the branches, shadows play,
A raccoon chased his pizza tray.
"You thief!" yelled out a nearby bird,
"That's not your snack, that's quite absurd!"

A lizard basked, in sunlight laid,
While pondering the pranks he played.
"My tail may twist, but my wit's quite keen,
Tomorrow I'll prank you, if you've not seen!"

A parade of ants marched proud and fast,
"We'll take this crumb and make it last!"
They bumped into a crab and laughed,
"We'll see whose pantry's truly half-staffed!"

Old leaves whispered, shook with glee,
At creatures cavorting, wild and free.
"Laughing echoes burst into the air,
Nature's jesters, without a single care!"

Steps in the Fading Green

Bouncing along a leafy trail,
Squirrels giggle, tell a tale.
A rabbit hops, a dance so spry,
While butterflies laugh, oh my!

Mushrooms wear hats in a row,
Toadstools tap, 'Come join the show!'
The path twists like a silly clown,
As squirrels serve snacks, a nutty crown.

Acorns drop like raindrops sweet,
Bouncing off my dancing feet.
The leaves clap hands, they cheer and spin,
A merry march, let the fun begin!

In fading green, we'll laugh and play,
Chasing shadows, bright and gay.
With every step, the joy will swell,
In the woods, it's a joke to tell!

Under the Embrace of Twilight

Beneath the sky where shadows tease,
Crickets chirp, as if to please.
Fireflies blink like weary stars,
They start a dance from Venus to Mars.

The owls hoot in a playful tone,
"Hey, listen up, we're not alone!"
A fox trips over his own proud tail,
"Who planned this party? I'll send a mail!"

The stars arrive in coats so bright,
"Can anyone join this funky night?"
Clouds make faces, puffed up with pride,
As giggles tremble on the wind's glide.

Under twilight's velvet dome,
We shout our secrets — "Take me home!"
But not before the raccoons sing,
To a waltz that makes the night take wing!

Hushed Voices among the Ferns

Amidst the fronds, some whispers start,
The ferns conspire with a leafy heart.
"Did you hear about the dandelion's new dress?
She's wearing sunshine, I must confess!"

A ladybug swings, twirling wide,
While a beetle claims, "I'm the bashful guide!"
They gossip softly, sharing a laugh,
As the shadows dance on the forest's path.

A woodpecker's knock is a rhythm divine,
"Hey, keep it down, that's my favorite line!"
The moss sways gently, full of delight,
As it joins the chatter beneath the moonlight.

With hushed voices, the woodland schemes,
In laughter and whispers, they share their dreams.
Each leaf a witness to this funny spree,
Nature's giggles, echoing free!

Love Letters to the Elder Oaks

Beneath the branches, thick and grand,
Whispers float like grains of sand.
The roots are tangled in comedy's tale,
While squirrels debate who's the fastest snail.

"Your bark is tough but your heart is dear,"
Squeaks a chipmunk, while munching a sphere.
The old oaks chuckle, their wisdom shared,
"This young cheekiness, well-prepared!"

With acorns dropping like little plans,
The trees conspire, forming new bands.
"Dear saplings, listen, lend us your ears,
For laughter shapes the best kind of cheers!"

They're love letters penned in rustling leaves,
Building up joy that never deceives.
In each crook and cranny, a story unfolds,
As humor's embrace in the forest holds.

Shadows of Solitude

In the thick of trees, I lost my way,
A squirrel stood guard, what did he say?
He chattered on, with quite the flair,
About acorns and nuts, his wealth to share.

Beneath the boughs, where silence reigns,
A raccoon danced, ignoring my pains.
With each silly twirl, he'd wink and smirk,
Was he the king of this forest work?

A rabbit peeked out with a cheeky grin,
'You lost, my friend, or trying to win?'
I shrugged and laughed, as they all sighed,
In this woodland world, it's fun to hide.

So if you wander, do take your time,
With giggles and pranks, nature's in rhyme.
For every corner's a joke or jest,
In this merry shade, we'll surely rest.

The Melody of Rustling Leaves

Leaves rustled low, with secrets they share,
The wind whistled tunes that were beyond compare.
A dove tried to sing, but forgot all the words,
So instead, she mumbled like bumbling birds.

The fox nearby chuckled, oh what a sound,
As he tried to dance, but fell to the ground.
His tail waved high, like a feathery flag,
Calling all critters to join in the brag.

A chorus of critters, quite out of tune,
Sang under the sun, and danced with the moon.
With giggles and hoots, they made quite a mess,
These silly old friends, a funny distress!

So hum along softly, when leaves sway and spin,
The laughter of nature invites you to join in.
Each rustle, each whisper, a jest in the air,
Where music and folly create a grand fair.

Beneath the Whispering Boughs

Beneath the trees where shadows play,
A hedgehog rolled by, in a spiny ballet.
He twirled on his back, with such silly grace,
Declaring this spot the best dancing place!

A squirrel flipped nuts, with imbalanced flair,
But tripped on a twig and fell in mid-air.
Laughter erupted from all nearby,
Even the flowers began to sigh.

Little bugs gathered, with a marvelous scene,
Fanning their wings, they all got so keen.
They spun round in circles, a dizzy parade,
While the old tree grumbled, "I'm getting less shade!"

Giggling and cackling, the forest became,
A stage for antics, delightful and tame.
So wander down paths with a smile on your face,
And remember, dear friend, it's a whimsical place.

A Tapestry Woven in Nature

A rabbit ran past with a tuft of green,
Trip over his feet? It's quite the routine!
He chuckled and grinned, 'What a sight to behold,'
As he fumbled and tumbled, so silly and bold.

An owl in the branches, a scholar so wise,
Slept through the ruckus, had dreams of a prize.
When finally waking, he blinked quite confused,
Said, 'What's all this nonsense? I was not amused.'

The flowers were chatting, their petals a-flutter,
Gossiping sweetly about who stepped in butter.
With every swirl, and a tickle of breeze,
The woods turned to laughter, bringing warmth with ease.

So next time you're lost, just laugh and look around,
For nature's the jester, in joy you are found.
With critters all joining, the fun never ends,
In this tapestry woven, with laughter, it bends.

Emblazoned with the Light of Dawn

A squirrel wearing a tiny hat,
Chased a butterfly and fell in a spat.
The sun peeked out with a golden grin,
While the raccoons were plotting to win.

A robin sang songs of breakfast delight,
As chipmunks performed their daring flight.
The breeze giggled, a ticklish breeze,
And teased the leaves with mischievous ease.

A hare did a jig on a mossy stone,
While frogs croaked rhymes in their secret tone.
With every twirl and leap of joy,
Nature's stage was set for every girl and boy.

The dawn painted smiles with its first glow,
As woodland creatures put on a show.
In this comedy of morning's embrace,
Life is a circus in this lively space.

The Silhouette of Silent Sentinels

Tall trees stand like watchers at night,
Dancing shadows join the moonlight.
An owl hooted, wearing a frown,
As a lost racoon wandered town to town.

The branches whispered secrets so old,
Of fairy tales bravely retold.
With each gusty laugh, the trunks would sway,
Telling the tales of a clumsy young jay.

The stars twinkled, pinpricks of glee,
While crickets chirped, 'come laugh with me!'
A badger slid down a slippy hill,
In a tumble of leaves, with a giggle and thrill.

The moon winked softly, shining its light,
On giggling shadows that danced with delight.
In this playful world, all worries evanesce,
As even the oak holds a toothy impress.

A Pilgrim's Reverie in Shades of Green

A wanderer strolled with a map upside down,
Drawing circles in grass, wearing a frown.
With every turn, he met a new friend,
An oddball parade that will never end.

A fern started arguing with a rock,
While a grasshopper strolled with an elegant clock.
Each blade chuckled, tickling his feet,
As mushrooms winked, oh, what a treat!

A hedgehog in tweed addressed the crowd,
Complaining about squirrels that always got loud.
With jests about acorns, the forest roared,
While the stream nearby seemed to applaud.

The warmth of the day spun stories like yarn,
As laughter echoed, not a single heart worn.
In shades of laughter and hues so refined,
Nature's comedy left no joy behind.

The Glimmer of Hidden Paths

On a path where the daisies twirled in delight,
A tortoise raced with all of its might.
They laughed at the flops of a clumsy small bee,
Who thought it could dance, oh how could it be!

A trail of snickers adorned every turn,
As mushrooms giggled, oh what fun to learn!
With whispers of breezes and teasing winds,
The forest was crafting some playful spins.

A wandering fox with a top hat so neat,
Offered a dance to each twinkling beat.
With twirls and bows that were less than precise,
Even owls joined in, oh once or twice!

Amidst the glimmers of paths hidden well,
Echoed laughter in a woodland spell.
With every step, joy sprouted anew,
In this land of fun, where spirits just flew.

Footprints of the Forest Spirits

In the woods, I saw a dance,
Squirrels pranced and took a chance.
With acorn hats, they twirled around,
While giggling trees whispered their sound.

One tree sighed, 'I lost my shoe!'
A rabbit laughed, 'I've lost one too!'
They searched beneath the leafy spread,
Found only mushrooms, and then they fled.

The mushrooms chuckled, sprouting high,
'You'd not find shoes beneath the sky!'
With every step, the forest groaned,
As spirits laughed—oh, jesters bowned!

So if you walk where shadows play,
Look for hats and shoes of clay.
For in this realm of playful sprites,
Every step could lead to bites!

Misty Mornings of Memory

A fog rolled in, quite thick and gray,
Where even ghosts have lost their way.
I strolled and tripped on murky roots,
And nearly landed in some boots!

A deer peeked out, its face so bold,
'You looking for your socks, I'm told!'
With a grin, it hopped and danced,
While misty echoes laughed, entranced.

The trees all chuckled, leaves a-shake,
'Don't look for socks, but for the lake!'
I spun around in playful haste,
And almost tumbled, what a waste!

Yet in the mist, a thought took flight,
Was it the deer or did I bite?
In every nook where shadows creak,
Misty mornings bring laughter, so to speak!

Adrift in the Swaying Green

Leaves above were waving 'hi,'
As I walked on, feeling spry.
A parrot squawked, 'What brings you here?'
'I'm looking for snacks!' I grinned with cheer.

The flowers giggled, petals bright,
'We have banana pie tonight!'
I danced along the grassy tide,
While ants all formed a tiny ride.

A tortoise blinked, 'Just take it slow,
A pie tastes better if you savor, you know?'
But by that time, I spied a bee,
And chased it off to join the spree!

In swaying glades, I laughed away,
With creatures who love to laugh and play.
Each rustling sound, a joke well-told,
In nature's arms, the joy unfolds!

Nature's Breath in the Glade

A breeze that tickles, a gentle tease,
Where butterflies float like subtle peas.
I tripped on roots, oh what a sight!
And startled a raccoon—a funny fright!

A squirrel chattered, 'Oh watch your step,
It's a dance of dirt, don't be inept!'
And in a swirl of autumn's grace,
I joined a conga line—not quite my pace!

The flowers joked, 'We just bloom and bow,
But you? You tumble like a cow!'
I rolled along, a giggling mess,
In this glade where laughter's the best!

So if you wander, just laugh and play,
Nature thrives when we let it sway.
With every fall, there's joy to greet,
In a world where mishaps dance to beat!

The Song of the Stillness

In the quiet, the squirrels plot,
They gossip about the strange robot.
Leafy hats and acorns galore,
Dance around, but trip on the floor.

A tune of rustles, a rhythm of cheer,
Crickets conspire, but no one will hear.
Laughter echoes from hollowed-out trees,
While owls chuckle at jokes on the breeze.

The shadows sway with a comical clap,
As the rabbits unite for a quick little nap.
They dream of carrots in fields unplanted,
While branches shift, feeling somewhat enchanted.

In stillness, the forest reveals its flair,
Where even the bushes flash mischievous hair.
A tickle of wind, and all pranks begin,
As the ducks waddle by in a zany spin.

A Journey into the Leafy Heart

The path is twisted, the leaves are bright,
A frog rides a snail, oh what a sight!
They hop along with a giggling cheer,
To find hidden treasures, but what's that near?

A gnome in pajamas, sipping his tea,
Wondering if this snail's quite speedy.
He shouts, "Hey, hurry! There's cake on the run!"
As the forest erupts in a ticklish pun.

A bear in a tutu joins for the feast,
Juggling berries with style, oh what a beast!
Squirrel stands guard near a mushroom-shaped throne,
While the forest applauds with a soft, grassy groan.

With donuts on branches, they all take a slice,
And a moment of laughter turns simple to nice.
This leafy journey, a comedic spree,
Where every small creature finds joy to be free.

Fables Written in Bark

Once upon a time, in a twisty old tree,
Lived a snail who swore he could swim in the sea!
He bobbed in a puddle, calling it shore,
While the frogs nearby laughed and begged him for more.

An ant with a crown planned a royal parade,
But the marchers tripped over a pile of jade.
As petals confetti flew up in the air,
The queen bug sighed, "Who put that there?"

Bees hummed a tune about golden delight,
But forgot the words midway through their flight.
They buzzed and they flapped, creating a show,
Until a spider spun webs, causing woe.

The bark held these tales, a riotous lore,
Of critters and giggles in folklore galore.
So next time you wander, just stop and remark,
For every good story is written in bark.

Cascading Sunbeams and Secrets

Sunbeams tumble, like kids at play,
Tickling the leaves in a bright, silly way.
A bumblebee buzzes, wearing a hat,
And a ladybug joins in, just like that!

They frolic in patches of shimmering light,
While shadows poke fun, but it's all in good sight.
A rabbit appears with a carrot so grand,
Proclaiming it's a treasure from a magical land!

The sun giggles softly, casting a grin,
As flowers start whispering secrets within.
A butterfly flutters, spreading wild cheer,
Joining the laughter that lingers near.

In this merry dance of the bright afternoon,
Nature throws parties to a whimsical tune.
So follow the rays and discover with glee,
The secrets concealed in the laughter of trees.

Trails Twisted by Time

There once was a trail, so twisted and tight,
It looped like a dancer, in pure delight.
The squirrels wore hats, and the rabbits did sway,
They threw a wild party, both night and day.

The trees, in a gossip, stood tall and bemused,
While a frog in a top hat felt thoroughly used.
With each little misstep, a giggle would break,
As chipmunks made puns about ice cream and cake.

The rocks were all raucous, they tumbled and rolled,
Claiming they'd once been great warriors bold.
"Now look at us, trapped, by the passersby!"
Cried one little stone, "Oh to fly or to die!"

But laughter grew louder, a contagious cheer,
For in every misstep, joy brought them near.
So next time you wander far down that lane,
Just join in the fun, and embrace all the pain!

Enchantment in the Emerald Depths

Deep in the green where the shadows play,
A cat in a cloak warned, "Beware of the fray!"
The rabbits wore glasses, quite scholarly breeds,
Debating the merits of magical seeds.

Mushrooms were dancing, in old-fashioned shoes,
Telling tall tales from forgotten blues.
"A wizard," they said, "danced upon a pie!"
As crows in bowties just chuckled nearby.

Frogs croaked like sirens with voices so bold,
While fireflies twinkled, their joy to unfold.
"Let's concoct a potion!" a brave badger cried,
While all of his friends just rolled eyes and sighed.

The laughter grew louder, as night filled the glen,
With whispers of stardust and tales without end.
So if you find magic in emerald glee,
Join in with the wonders, there's room for thee!

Voices Carried on the Breeze

In the crisp air, a whisper danced light,
A squirrel named Benny soared into flight.
With acorns in hand, he'd dart here and there,
While passing a tale on the soft summer air.

The trees leaned in close, ears perked and alert,
To catch every story, each giggle, each flirt.
"I saw a bear wearing a tutu!" he cheered,
While birds dropped their muffins, astonished and weird.

Up floated a breeze, with pirates in tow,
Claiming they'd buried a treasure of snow.
But the snowmen all melted, the tale turned to sand,
Leaving giggles behind on this whimsical land.

So if ever you hear a laugh in the air,
It's Benny the squirrel, now swinging with flair.
Just listen and smile, for joy's all around,
With voices that dance in the softest of sound!

Secrets of the Gnarled Branches

Gnarled branches whisper, with secrets to share,
About a nut thief who scampers with flair.
The owl's got gossip, the fox has the scoop,
Of acorns and antics in their quirky troop.

"Did you see that raccoon with a hat made of twigs?"
The trees rustled softly, "He's plotting for gigs!"
While hedgehogs exchanged their best fashion tips,
As turtles declared it was "last year's eclipse."

Now and then, a butterfly winked from its perch,
While crickets danced wildly, oh what a search!
"Do we have enough zest for this lively affair?"
And the bushes all jeered, in a dirty old chair.

In shadows, they gather, these creatures so spry,
With laughter and mischief flying high to the sky.
Secrets exchanged, in the hush of the leaves,
In the heart of their woodland, where humor believes!

Memories Carved in Wood

Squirrels chatter with a cheeky grin,
While turtles tumble, looking for kin.
A raccoon plays the drums on a log,
As a nearby frog croaks out a dialogue.

Bark is scratched with stories untold,
By mice wearing capes, brave and bold.
They giggle and dance under the sun,
In their world, every day's full of fun.

A wooden sign points the silly way,
To dance parties held at the end of the day.
Pinecones fall like confetti galore,
Each laugh echoes, begging for more.

Echoes of laughter whisper by
Where leaves pirouette and twigs fly high.
Nature's jesters create the mood,
In this merry, enchanted wood.

A Dawn's Embrace in Cobalt

The sun peeks in, the bluebirds cheer,
While raccoons brush their fur to look clear.
A deer juggles acorns with great flair,
As a fox struts by with a stylish air.

Morning mist hugs the trees so tight,
While chipmunks debate if they'll take flight.
A frog wears a crown made of dewdrops,
While bees in tiaras do syrupy hops.

The cobalt sky sparkles like a joke,
As owls laugh softly, enjoying the smoke.
Spinning tales of the night on their perch,
With giggles that echo, they begin their lurch.

Every twig creaks with a whiny tune,
As sunbeams dance to a comical croon.
Nature's slapstick in bright sunny rays,
Bringing giggles to greet the morning haze.

The Light's Whisper in the Canopy

Sunbeams peek through leafy hats,
As shadows hide the giggling spats.
A squirrel slides down a slippery vine,
    Chasing after a whispering pine.

Branches sway like they're in a dance,
While bunnies zoom by in a hop and prance.
A woodpecker insists on a knock-knock joke,
    Bursts of laughter ripple as folks provoke.

The canopy hums with stories once spun,
    As fireflies twinkle, declaring it fun.
Moss carpets the ground, a plush delight,
Where snails sip tea and dine at twilight.

Every rustle is filled with delight,
As woodland critters share their insight.
Laughter and whispers blend in the air,
    In this silly place, without a care.

The Forest's Quiet Legacy

Old trees reminisce with a creaky laugh,
While an ant conducts a bug symphony staff.
Underneath roots, stories gently unfold,
Of creatures both silly and brave and bold.

A snail tells tales of adventures far,
While beetles boast of the best cookie jar.
Nature's comedy played out in bright hues,
As flowers laugh along, sharing their views.

Each whispering leaf adds its own bit,
To the merry songs that the crickets emit.
Slowly dancing, shadows skip and twirl,
As the forest giggles in mirth's swirl.

Legacy lives in echoes of cheer,
Singing sweet soliloquies all can hear.
In this playful woodland, filled with glee,
The forest's heartbeats sing joyfully free.

Whispers of the Wandering Breeze

There's a squirrel that tells tall tales,
Nibbling acorns and waving its sails.
With every gust, it spins a new yarn,
Of knights and dragons 'neath trees so worn.

A raccoon chuckles, perched on a branch,
As he stirs the leaves in a merry dance.
"What's that? A joke? Oh, do tell me more!"
Together they giggle by the old forest's door.

Even the brook has a gurgling laugh,
As fish tell secrets, each drawing a graph.
Make way for the breeze, it's got stories to spin,
While the fungi debate if they're lost or they win.

So listen up, friends, and lend an ear,
The woods are alive with humor and cheer.
From the whispering leaves to the twitching tails,
Life in this realm never ever pales.

Saplings Speak in Secret Tongues

Little saplings gossip at night,
Sharing secrets with the moon's soft light.
"Did you see that owl stumble and trip?"
"Oh yes! He landed right on his hip!"

Mossy mounds chuckle, shaking their heads,
As worms trade jokes while hiding in beds.
"Why did the beetle cross the way?"
"To find a good snack, or just to play!"

The ferns flutter like they've got a scheme,
Whispering softly, as if in a dream.
"If only the wind could carry our fun,"
"We'd be the jesters 'til the day is done!"

Sprites hide behind trunks, laughing and peeking,
At the tales of the trees, who keep on speaking.
Each rustle and shuffle, a comedic delight,
In the world where the saplings find voice in the night.

Muffled Truths of the Woodland Heart

In the woodland, where shadows play tag,
Lies a notion wrapped in each humble snag.
A hedgehog snorts with a laugh profound,
"I'm not just cute, I'm the wisest around!"

Crickets chirp riddles from dark leafy cracks,
While fireflies flash like tiny old hacks.
"What glows in the dark but hides in plain sight?"
"A lamp that forgot it's still daytime bright!"

The trees lean closer to hear the latest,
As branches swag and bark reveals traits.
"Truth's just a whisper, or so they say,
Unless you're a bird with too much to relay!"

So gather 'round, for the woodland's smart,
With every chortle, it nudges the heart.
As muffled laughter spreads through the glade,
The secrets of trees and critters invade.

A Tapestry of Twilit Faces

In twilight's embrace, a canvas unfolds,
With chuckles and giggles, a story retolds.
Frogs in top hats croak silly debate,
While hedgehogs play cards, and postulate fate.

Rabbits prance lightly, with feathers in tow,
Dancing on mushrooms, putting on shows.
"What's a vampire's favorite kind of fruit?"
"A neck-a-rine! Oh, ain't that a hoot!"

The owls roll their eyes, wise as can be,
As they watch the frolics of folly run free.
Each face in the gathering wears a bright grin,
In this tapestry rich with the joyfulness within.

So linger a moment in dusk's gentle charm,
Where laughter and whimsy create the warm.
In a world where absurdity never shall cease,
Nature's funny tales bring the heart sweet peace.

Starlit Trails and Hidden Dreams

Underneath the twinkling skies,
The squirrels hold a grand surprise.
They dance around in silly styles,
While owls roll their eyes and smile.

Beneath the trees, a shadow dashes,
A raccoon boasts of daring clashes.
He claims to lift the moon so bright,
But trips and falls—oh, what a sight!

The fireflies trying to compete,
With glowworms who can't feel their feet.
They jitterbug and spin in glee,
While giggling softly—"Look at me!"

In midnight waltzes, trees sway low,
With branches dancing to and fro.
The laughter echoes, wild and free,
In nature's joyful jubilee.

Whispers Among the Ferns

Among the ferns, a chatter starts,
As rabbits play their wooden arts.
They build a fort, but it's a flop,
When one leapt high and made a plop.

The turtles talk of speed and grace,
While slipping in a muddy race.
They boast of rivals, quick and sly,
But turtle jokes can't help but fly.

A caterpillar with a hat,
Proclaims he's bold—just look at that!
He struts around to show his flair,
But gets caught down—oh, what a scare!

With whispers soft, the secrets spread,
Of plants that dream of all things red.
They giggle under leafy screens,
And scheme quite silly, no in-betweens.

Dancing Flames of the Forest

In the glade where shadows dance,
The campfire flames start a romance.
They sway and jiggle, bright and quick,
While shyly flirting with a stick.

The logs begin a slow two-step,
As crickets jump and try to pep.
They chirp a tune, but meet their fate,
When fireflies join to elevate.

The shadows giggle as they spin,
As raccoons step in with a grin.
They juggle nuts upon their heads,
While owls hoot loud from their beds.

With twinkling flames, the night grows bold,
As secrets of the woods unfold.
All join in laughter, wild and warm,
In this lively, glowing swarm.

The Twilight's Gentle Embrace

In twilight's glow, the critters meet,
The hedgehogs roll, oh what a feat!
They stumble in a happy mess,
Like furry balls in tuxedo dress.

The frogs compete in croaking tunes,
While beetles dance beneath the moons.
They flaunt their moves, a funny game,
With wobbly waltzes, none the same.

A raccoon with cookies, none to share,
Claims they're secret—beware, beware!
But as he turns, they slip and fall,
His cookie jar—oh dear, how small!

With giggles bright, the night proceeds,
As nature hums her rhythmic deeds.
In silky hugs, the forest gleams,
A tapestry of silly dreams.

www.ingramcontent.com/pod-product-compliance
Lightning Source LLC
Chambersburg PA
CBHW071846160426
43209CB00003B/439